W9-BIH-457

From:
Little Lambs
Elmhurst Chr. Ref. Church

Loving Is...

by Janet Gonter

illustrated by Lyn Seward

STANDARD PUBLISHING
Cincinnati, Ohio 3604

Library of Congress Cataloging-in-Publication Data

Gonter, Janet.
  Loving is—.

  Summary: A young child discovers that there are many
different ways to say "I love you."
  1. Love—Religious aspects—Christianity—Juvenile
literature. [1. Love, 2, Christian life]
I. Seward, Lyn, ill. II. Title.
BV4639.G665 1986   248.8'2   86-5711
ISBN 0-87403-124-9

Loving Is...

I'm around lots of people everyday—friends, family, and neighbors. I know Jesus wants me to love everyone, but sometimes it's hard for me to say the words, "I love you." Maybe I can say "I love you" by the things I *do* instead.

I can say "I love you" to my mother by ...

setting the table for her.

cleaning my room without being told.

I can say "I love you" to my daddy by ...

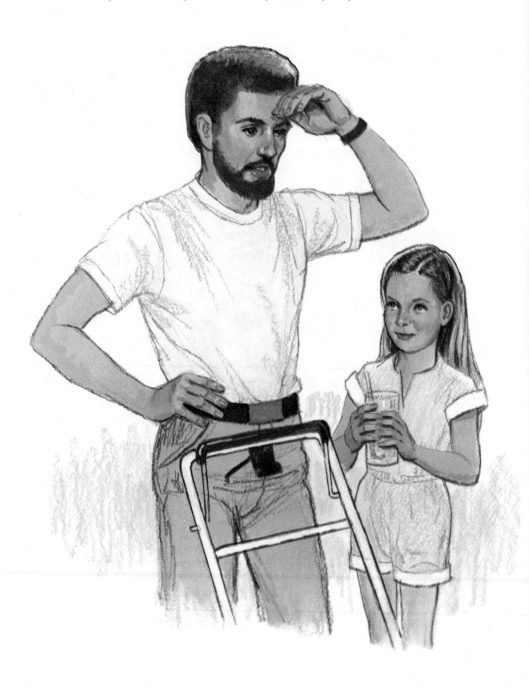

bringing him iced tea when he's cutting the grass.

getting tools for him when he's busy fixing
something.

I can say "I love you" to my grandmother by...

painting her a picture and sending it in the mail.

giving her an extra hug.

I can say "I love you" to my grandfather by ...

helping mother bake his favorite pie.

asking him to tell me about when he was
little.

I can say "I love you" to my little sister by ...

saving the last cookie for her.

letting her come into my bed when she's
scared.

I can say "I love you" to my big brother by . . .

cheering when he hits a home run.

keeping his secrets, and being his friend.

I can say "I love you" to my Sunday-school teacher by ...

being a good listener.

holding the door for her.

I can say "I love you" to the older people on my street by ...

shoveling snow from their sidewalk, even if I'm not asked.

asking them if they need anything at the
store.

I can say "I love you" to the meanest kid I know by ...

inviting him to Sunday school.

asking him if he wants to play baseball.

I can say "I love you" to my neighbors by ...

watering their flowers while they're away.

keeping my friends out of their yard.

I can say "I love you" to my best friend by . . .

caring when she's sad.

being happy when something good happens
to her.

I can say "I love you" to everyone I meet by ...
treating them the way I would like to be
treated.

It's fun to say "I love you" by doing nice things for people. It makes them happy, and that makes me happy. I think Jesus likes that.